The Secret of Positive and Successful Mindset

Building a Champion's Mind

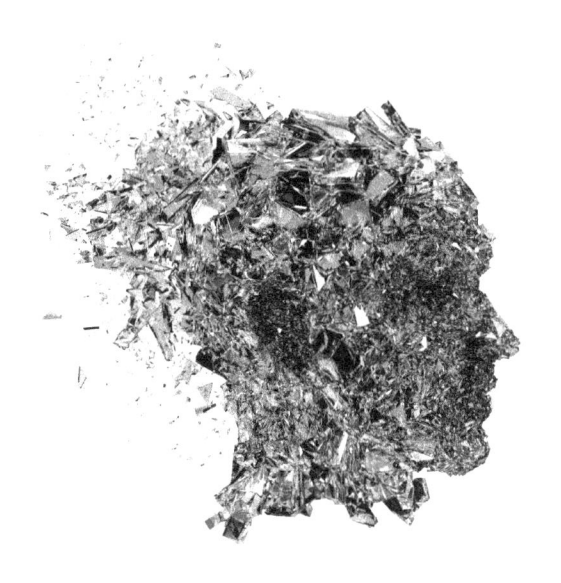

Unlocking Your Potential
Embrace Repetition to Achieve Greatness

Lucas Oliver Williams

Copyright ©2023 Lucas Oliver Williams
All rights reserved.

Reproduction of any content in this publication is strictly prohibited unless written permission is obtained from the publisher. The only exception is for brief quotes included in critical articles or reviews. The photos used in the book are licensed under Canva Pro.

INTRODUCTION

Welcome to "The Secret of Positive and Successful Mindset"! In this transformative journey, we embark on an exploration of the extraordinary power that lies within each of us—a power that can shape our destinies and unlock the doors to success and fulfillment. At the heart of this empowering quest is the realization that our mindset holds the key to unlocking our true potential and achieving greatness.

A positive and successful mindset is not a fleeting notion or a mere stroke of luck; rather, it is a deliberate and purposeful state of being that we can nurture and cultivate. This book is designed to be your guide, providing you with the tools and exercises necessary to embrace the principles of repetition, mindfulness, and positive beliefs to transform your life in profound ways.

Part I of the book will lay a strong foundation for your journey, as we delve into the fundamental concepts of positive mindset, repetition, and mindfulness. We will explore the science behind the remarkable ability of repetition to rewire our thought patterns, and how mindfulness can foster awareness and presence, unlocking the door to lasting change.

By understanding the interplay between our thoughts and actions, we will uncover how our mindset can influence our success, happiness, and overall well-being. Through introspective exercises, we will identify limiting beliefs that might have held us back, and learn to replace them with empowering and transformative affirmations.

Part II of "The Secret of Positive and Successful Mindset" is your dedicated exercise book—a treasure trove of repetitive phrases and affirmations meticulously crafted to target specific areas of your life. These exercises will become your daily companions on your journey to greatness, providing you with the building blocks to construct a mindset that supports and nurtures your dreams and aspirations.

Whether you seek to boost your self-confidence, attract abundance, overcome challenges, or cultivate meaningful relationships, the exercises in this book will equip you with the mental tools to achieve your goals. Remember, it is not just the repetition of words, but the unwavering belief in their truth, that can harness the full potential of your mind.

As you progress through the pages, be patient with yourself. Changing long-held beliefs and ingrained thought patterns may take time, but with commitment, dedication, and the gentle repetition of these exercises, you will witness the gradual transformation of your mindset—one that is resilient, positive, and open to the limitless possibilities that life has to offer.

So, let us embark together on this empowering journey of self-discovery, as we unlock the secrets of the mind and unleash the untapped potential within us. May "The Secret of Positive and Successful Mindset" be your trusted companion, guiding you towards a life of abundance, fulfillment, and unwavering success.

Are you ready to embrace the power of repetition and witness the magic it can bring into your life? Let's begin this extraordinary adventure, one page at a time.

Part 1

GROWTH MINDSET

The Role of Mindset in Success

Exploring the Impact of Mindset on Achievements

In the grand tapestry of human potential, the true determinant of success lies not solely in external circumstances but rather within the intricate workings of the mind. Our mindset, the lens through which we perceive the world and ourselves, plays a pivotal role in shaping the course of our achievements. The beliefs we hold about our abilities, our resilience in the face of challenges, and our receptiveness to growth all intertwine to chart the trajectory of our lives.

As we embark on this journey to unlock the secrets of a positive and successful mindset, it is crucial to understand the profound influence our mindset wields over our actions and outcomes. Picture your mindset as the foundation upon which the edifice of your life is built—the blueprint that either propels you to great heights or constrains you within self-imposed limitations.

A fixed mindset perceives abilities and talents as innate and unchangeable traits. People with a fixed mindset tend to believe that their intelligence, talents, and skills are predetermined, leading them to shy away from challenges that may risk exposing perceived weaknesses. Fear of failure becomes a formidable barrier, as it threatens to define their self-worth and identity.

Conversely, a growth mindset embraces the belief that abilities can be developed through dedication, effort, and a willingness to learn. Those with a growth mindset view challenges as opportunities for growth and see failures as stepping stones on the path to success. Embracing a growth mindset empowers individuals to take on new challenges, learn from setbacks, and persist in the face of adversity.

The impact of mindset on achievements becomes apparent when we observe two individuals with similar backgrounds and talents pursue different paths in life. One may flourish and surpass expectations, while the other remains stagnant, forever caught in the shadows of untapped potential. The defining factor often lies in the mindset they choose to adopt.

Consider this: A person with a fixed mindset might avoid applying for a dream job, fearing they lack the inherent abilities required for success. On the other hand, an individual with a growth mindset would eagerly seize the opportunity, viewing the job as a chance to develop new skills and excel in uncharted territory. The results of their endeavors are likely to reflect the mindset they embraced—the difference between remaining stagnant and embarking on a journey of growth and accomplishment.

Fortunately, our mindset is not set in stone. It is malleable, susceptible to change, and responsive to intentional efforts. By recognizing the patterns of our thoughts and the beliefs that underpin our actions, we can take charge of our mindset's direction and steer it towards a more positive and success-oriented course.

In the pages that follow, we will explore the transformative power of repetition—a technique that allows us to rewire our thought patterns and replace limiting beliefs with empowering affirmations. Additionally, we will delve into the practice of mindfulness, which enables us to cultivate a heightened awareness of our thoughts and emotions, fostering an environment conducive to lasting change.

Remember, success is not reserved for a select few; it is a journey accessible to all who dare to embrace the potential within themselves. As we equip ourselves with the knowledge and tools to cultivate a growth mindset, let us break free from the confines of self-imposed limitations and embrace a path of continuous growth, resilience, and fulfillment.

Together, let us unravel the secrets of the mind and awaken to the boundless possibilities that await us on this remarkable voyage toward a positive and successful mindset.

The Science of Repetition

How Repetition Shapes Beliefs and Behaviors

Repetition, an unassuming yet powerful force, weaves its way through the fabric of human cognition, leaving an indelible mark on our beliefs, behaviors, and ultimately, the course of our lives. This remarkable phenomenon lies at the core of how we learn, adapt, and evolve as individuals. As we delve into the science of repetition, we uncover the intricacies of its influence on our minds and the potential it holds for transformative change.

At its essence, repetition is the act of revisiting a thought, action, or experience multiple times, reinforcing neural pathways within the intricate web of our brains. Each repetition strengthens these pathways, making them more accessible and easier to traverse in the future. This mechanism of reinforcement lies at the heart of how repetition shapes our beliefs and behaviors.

When we repeatedly expose ourselves to certain ideas or concepts, they begin to take root in our subconscious mind, gradually permeating our conscious awareness. Over time, these beliefs become deeply ingrained, influencing our perceptions of ourselves, others, and the world around us. Positive and empowering beliefs, when consistently reinforced, can bolster our self-confidence and drive us towards success. Conversely, negative and limiting beliefs can shackle us, holding us back from reaching our full potential.

Consider a budding musician who diligently practices playing the guitar every day. With each practice session, the neural connections responsible for finger dexterity and musical memory are reinforced. As the musician continues to repeat these actions, playing becomes more fluid and effortless. The brain adapts to the repetition, optimizing its networks for the task at hand. This is an illustration of how repetition can enhance skill development and expertise, highlighting the remarkable plasticity of the human brain.

This brings us to the fascinating concept of neuroplasticity—the brain's extraordinary ability to reorganize and rewire itself in response to new experiences, learning, and repeated actions. Far from being fixed and unchangeable, the brain remains dynamic and adaptable throughout our lives. This plasticity allows us to learn from our environment, adapt to challenges, and forge new pathways that align with our intentions and aspirations.

The brain's adaptability is particularly significant when it comes to modifying our beliefs and mindset. By consciously engaging in repetitive exercises and affirmations, we can reshape the neural networks that underpin our thoughts, emotions, and behaviors. Over time, these new connections gain strength, and the beliefs they represent become an integral part of our self-concept.

Neuroplasticity serves as the bridge between repetition and lasting change. Embracing a growth mindset, where we believe in our capacity to evolve and improve, opens up vast possibilities for transformation. By repeatedly reinforcing positive thoughts and affirmations, we harness the brain's ability to adapt and forge new pathways, making it easier to embrace a more positive and successful mindset.

As we progress through this journey of discovery, remember that repetition is not a fleeting fix but a deliberate and consistent practice. Just as a sculptor chips away at a block of stone to reveal a masterpiece, we, too, mold our minds through repetition to shape a mindset that empowers us to thrive and conquer the challenges that life presents.

Together, let us uncover the wonders of repetition and witness its profound impact on our beliefs, behaviors, and the boundless potential that awaits us. Armed with this knowledge, we stand poised to unlock the secrets of a positive and successful mindset, paving the way for a life of fulfillment, growth, and endless possibilities.

Embracing Mindfulness

What Mindfulness Is and Its Connection to a Positive Mindset

In a world often filled with the cacophony of distractions and the frenetic pace of modern living, mindfulness emerges as a beacon of tranquility—a way to ground ourselves in the present moment and cultivate a deeper connection to our inner selves. This practice of being fully aware and attentive to the here and now has the power to transform our perceptions, thoughts, and emotions, establishing a profound connection to a positive mindset.

At its core, mindfulness is the art of non-judgmental awareness—a gentle observation of our thoughts, sensations, and emotions as they arise, without becoming entangled in their narratives. It encourages us to be fully present, without dwelling on the past or projecting into the future, allowing us to savor the richness of each passing moment. By anchoring ourselves in the present, we liberate our minds from the burdens of regrets and anxieties, creating space for clarity, calm, and self-acceptance.

The connection between mindfulness and a positive mindset is woven through the fabric of our cognitive and emotional processes. As we become mindful observers of our thoughts, we can recognize patterns of negativity, self-doubt, and limiting beliefs that may hinder our growth. Mindfulness helps us detach from these unhelpful thoughts, preventing them from dictating our actions and reactions.

Through the lens of mindfulness, we become more attuned to our emotional landscape, acknowledging our feelings without suppressing or indulging them. By embracing our emotions with acceptance and compassion, we learn to navigate life's challenges with greater resilience and understanding. As a result, a positive mindset emerges—a mindset that perceives setbacks as opportunities for growth, and challenges as stepping stones on the path to success.

Practicing Mindfulness in Daily Life

While mindfulness can be cultivated through formal meditation practices, its true essence lies in its integration into our daily lives. We need not retreat to a mountaintop or a secluded sanctuary to practice mindfulness. Instead, we can weave it into the fabric of our everyday experiences, transforming the mundane into moments of awareness and gratitude.

Begin by grounding yourself in the present moment. Whether you're sipping a cup of tea, walking in nature, or engaging in routine tasks, bring your attention to the sensations, sounds, and sights around you. Notice the warmth of the tea cup against your palms, the rustle of leaves underfoot, or the colors that paint the world.

As you interact with others, practice active listening—giving your undivided attention to the person speaking without interrupting or allowing your mind to drift. Truly hearing and understanding others fosters deeper connections and promotes empathy, enriching both your relationships and your own sense of well-being.

In moments of stress or overwhelm, turn to mindfulness as a refuge. Take a pause, close your eyes, and focus on your breath. Inhale deeply, feeling the air filling your lungs, and then exhale, releasing tension and worries with each breath. This simple act of mindful breathing can center and ground you, providing clarity and perspective in the face of challenges.

Mindfulness extends beyond the self to the world we inhabit. Engage in acts of kindness and compassion towards others, recognizing the interconnectedness of all beings. By nurturing empathy and understanding, we foster an environment of positivity and harmony.

Through consistent practice, mindfulness becomes an inherent part of who we are, permeating our thoughts, actions, and interactions with the world. It nurtures a positive mindset, one that embraces the beauty of the present moment, celebrates the potential for growth, and radiates a profound sense of gratitude and contentment.

As we navigate the pages that follow, let us remember that mindfulness is not an elusive goal but an accessible and transformative practice. Embrace mindfulness as a lifelong companion, guiding you towards a positive and successful mindset—one that thrives in the splendor of the present and flourishes in the boundless potential of tomorrow.

Setting Your Mindset Goals

Defining Your Vision for Success and Happiness

In the grand tapestry of life, our mindset acts as the master weaver, shaping the patterns and colors of our experiences. As we delve into the exercise book of "The Secret of Positive and Successful Mindset," let us take a moment to set our intentions and chart a course towards the life we aspire to create—a life abundant in success, happiness, and fulfillment.

To embark on this transformative journey, we must first define our vision for success and happiness. Consider what success truly means to you, beyond the confines of societal expectations. Reflect on the aspects of life that bring you joy and fulfillment—the passions that ignite a fire within your soul. Envision the person you wish to become, the accomplishments you aspire to achieve, and the impact you desire to make on the world.

As we paint this vivid portrait of our ideal life, we are drawn closer to the canvas of our dreams, ready to wield the brush of belief and determination. By setting clear and compelling mindset goals, we breathe life into our aspirations, empowering ourselves to take deliberate steps towards their realization.

Identifying Limiting Beliefs to Overcome

Just as a garden flourishes when cleared of weeds, our minds thrive when we identify and uproot limiting beliefs. These insidious thoughts, often sown by past experiences or external influences, can hinder our progress and impede the blossoming of our true potential.

With a mindful and compassionate eye, examine the beliefs that may have held you back in the past. Are there thoughts that undermine your self-confidence or reinforce a fixed mindset? By acknowledging these limiting beliefs, we loosen their grip on our psyche, creating space for empowering affirmations to take root.

As we transition into Part 2 of the book, where the exercise book awaits, let us embrace the transformative power of repetition to cultivate a fertile mindset—one that nurtures positivity, resilience, and boundless possibilities. Each exercise in the following pages serves as a stepping stone on the path to self-discovery, growth, and the unleashing of your full potential.

Part 2

GROWTH MINDSET

The Exercise Book

Within these pages lies a treasure trove of exercises, carefully crafted to address various aspects of life. Each chapter focuses on specific themes, designed to empower you with repetitive phrases that will gradually reshape your beliefs and behaviors.

As you engage with these exercises, remember that the magic lies not only in the words you repeat but in the unwavering faith you place in their transformative power. Embrace these exercises as daily rituals of empowerment—moments of quiet reflection and affirmations that will infuse your mind with the positivity and resilience needed to embrace challenges and flourish in all aspects of life.

Each exercise is an invitation to explore the vast landscape of your inner world, to discover the vast reservoir of potential that resides within you. Allow yourself to be vulnerable and open to the possibilities of growth. There is no judgment here, only gentle encouragement to nurture the seeds of positivity and watch them bloom into a life of purpose, joy, and accomplishment.

As we venture through the chapters of the exercise book, let us embark on this journey together—the journey of unlocking the secret of a positive and successful mindset. With every phrase repeated, we etch the blueprint of transformation upon the canvas of our minds, one stroke at a time.

Are you ready to embark on this empowering adventure of self-discovery? Let the exercise book be your guide, leading you towards a mindset that thrives on the foundation of repetition, mindfulness, and the unwavering belief in the power of your dreams. Let us begin this extraordinary voyage, embracing the boundless potential that lies ahead, as we set sail towards a life filled with positivity, success, and fulfillment.

Chapter of Self-Love

Repetitive Phrases for Cultivating Self-Compassion and Self-Worth

In the beautiful landscape of our minds, self-love is the gentle rain that nurtures the seeds of self-compassion and self-worth. It is a powerful elixir that allows us to embrace our imperfections, celebrate our uniqueness, and honor the journey of self-discovery we embark upon. Within this chapter lies a collection of repetitive phrases—words that will wrap you in a warm embrace of love and acceptance, empowering you to cultivate a profound sense of self-compassion and embrace your inherent worth.

Exercise 1: Embracing My Authentic Self

"I love and accept myself unconditionally, just as I am."
"My worth is not defined by external standards; I am enough."
"I honor my journey, with all its ups and downs, as it has shaped who I am today."

Exercise 2: Letting Go of Self-Judgment

"I release all self-criticism and embrace self-compassion."
"I forgive myself for past mistakes; they do not define my future."
"I replace judgment with kindness, recognizing that I am only human."

Exercise 3: Nurturing My Inner Child

"I cherish the child within me and shower them with love and care."
"I give myself permission to play, explore, and experience joy."
"I am deserving of love and tenderness, just as any child is."

Exercise 4: Setting Boundaries and Prioritizing My Needs

"I honor my boundaries and communicate them with confidence."
"My needs are important and worthy of being met."
"I prioritize self-care, as it replenishes my mind, body, and soul."

Exercise 5: Affirming My Uniqueness

"I celebrate my uniqueness and embrace my individuality."
"I shine bright as my authentic self, without comparing to others."
"My quirks and differences are what make me special and remarkable."

Exercise 6: Embracing Positive Affirmations

"I am worthy of love, success, and happiness."
"I believe in myself and my abilities to overcome any challenge."
"I am deserving of all the good that life has to offer."

Exercise 7: Practicing Gratitude for Myself

"I am grateful for the person I am becoming, and I embrace my growth."
"I acknowledge my strengths and the progress I've made on my journey."
"I am a gift to myself and to the world around me."

Exercise 8: Letting Love Guide My Choices

"I make choices that reflect self-love and compassion."
"I prioritize relationships that uplift and nourish my soul."
"I surround myself with love and let go of anything that no longer serves me."

As you repeat these phrases, allow their essence to seep into the depths of your being. Embrace them with an open heart, for they are not mere words; they are the seeds of self-love that, with each repetition, will bloom into a profound sense of self-compassion and self-worth. In moments of doubt or struggle, return to these phrases as a guiding light, illuminating your path towards a profound and unwavering love for the beautiful soul that you are.

Let the practice of self-love become a daily ritual—an act of kindness you gift to yourself. In nurturing your relationship with yourself, you pave the way for deeper connections with others and the world around you. Remember, your capacity to love and be loved begins within your own heart. As you cultivate self-compassion and embrace your worth, you become a beacon of love, radiating positivity and touching the lives of those around you.

Embrace this transformative chapter of self-love, and let the repetitive phrases be the gentle rain that nurtures the seeds of compassion and worth within you. Together, let us bask in the warmth of self-love and celebrate the journey of self-discovery as we continue to unveil the secrets of a positive and successful mindset.

Chapter of Gratitude

Exercises to Enhance Gratitude and Attract Abundance

Gratitude, a magical elixir that infuses our lives with richness and joy, holds the power to transform the ordinary into the extraordinary. In this chapter, we embark on a journey of cultivating gratitude—a practice that opens our hearts to the abundance that surrounds us and invites more blessings into our lives. Through a series of exercises, we will nurture the spirit of gratitude within us, fostering a profound appreciation for life's blessings, big and small.

Exercise 1: Gratitude Journaling

Take a few moments each day to reflect on the things you are grateful for and jot them down in your gratitude journal. Whether it's a loving relationship, a fulfilling accomplishment, or a simple act of kindness, acknowledging and recording these moments of gratitude will deepen your sense of appreciation and create a positive outlook on life.

Exercise 2: Gratitude Walks

Embark on a gratitude walk, immersing yourself in nature's beauty. As you stroll, mindfully observe the wonders around you—the vibrant colors of flowers, the gentle rustling of leaves, or the sun's warmth on your skin. Express gratitude for the beauty of the natural world and the privilege of being a part of it.

Exercise 3: Gratitude Affirmations

Repeat gratitude affirmations daily to cultivate a mindset of abundance and thankfulness. Let these phrases resonate within your heart:

"I am grateful for the abundance that flows into my life."
"I attract blessings and opportunities with an open heart and grateful spirit."
"I appreciate the gifts that life presents to me, big and small."

Exercise 4: Gratitude Letters

Write heartfelt letters of gratitude to those who have touched your life in meaningful ways. Express your appreciation for their presence, support, or acts of kindness. Sending these letters or reading them in person can deepen your connections and nurture a sense of gratitude within your relationships.

Exercise 5: Gratitude Meditation

Engage in a gratitude meditation, where you focus on feelings of thankfulness and appreciation. Breathe deeply, and with each breath, envision a sense of gratitude growing within your heart. Feel the warmth of gratitude radiate through your being, embracing the present moment with acceptance and contentment.

Exercise 6: Gratitude Jar

Create a gratitude jar, where you place notes of thanks for the blessings you encounter throughout each day. At the end of the week or month, take a moment to read these notes and relish in the abundance of positivity that surrounds you.

Exercise 7: Gratitude Sharing

In conversations with loved ones or friends, consciously share moments of gratitude. Encourage each other to express appreciation for the blessings in your lives, creating a supportive atmosphere of thankfulness and joy.

As you immerse yourself in these exercises, allow the spirit of gratitude to become a constant companion in your life. The more you embrace gratitude, the more blessings you attract and the more you recognize the abundance that exists within and around you.

Let this chapter be a portal to a life of gratitude—a life that overflows with appreciation for the present and hope for the future. Embrace the magic of gratitude, for in its embrace, you'll discover that abundance resides not just in the grand milestones but also in the intricacies of everyday life. As you cultivate gratitude, you open the doors to endless possibilities, inviting a world of abundance and fulfillment into your life.

Chapter of Affirmations for Success

Repetition Techniques to Build Confidence and Foster Success

Within the realm of our thoughts lies the blueprint for success—the seeds of greatness waiting to be nurtured. Affirmations, like the rays of the sun, provide the warmth and light that awaken these seeds, empowering us to grow with confidence and purpose. In this chapter, we delve into the world of affirmations—a powerful tool for cultivating a positive mindset and unlocking our potential for success.

Exercise 1: Affirmations for Self-Confidence

"I am capable and competent in all that I do."
"I trust in my abilities to overcome challenges with grace and determination."
"I believe in myself and my unique talents, and I let go of self-doubt."

Exercise 2: Affirmations for Goal Achievement

"I set clear and achievable goals, and I pursue them relentlessly."
"With each step I take, I move closer to the realization of my dreams."
"I attract success and opportunities that align with my vision."

Exercise 3: Affirmations for Resilience

"I face adversity with strength and resilience."
"Challenges are stepping stones to my growth and success."
"I rise above setbacks, knowing they are temporary and valuable lessons."

Exercise 4: Affirmations for Positive Thinking

"I attract positivity and abundance into my life."
"I focus on the solutions rather than dwelling on problems."
"My thoughts are optimistic and align with my vision for success."

Exercise 5: Affirmations for Creativity

"I embrace my unique creativity, and it flows effortlessly through me."
"I am open to new ideas and inspirations that lead to innovation and success."
"My creative potential is boundless, and I express it with confidence."

Exercise 6: Affirmations for Taking Action

"I am proactive and take bold steps towards my goals."
"I seize opportunities fearlessly, knowing they lead to growth and achievement."
"I am the architect of my destiny, and I create my own success."

Exercise 7: Affirmations for Attracting Abundance

"I am deserving of abundance and prosperity."
"Opportunities for success surround me, and I seize them with gratitude."
"I welcome wealth and abundance into my life, knowing they serve my highest good."

Exercise 8: Affirmations for Embracing Growth

"I am committed to my personal growth and development."
"I welcome change as an opportunity for positive transformation."
"With each new challenge, I become a better version of myself."

As you repeat these affirmations, feel their resonance within your heart and mind. Embrace them as truth, for they reflect the powerful potential that resides within you. With each repetition, you build a strong foundation of self-belief and positive energy that will propel you towards your desired success.

Integrate these affirmations into your daily routine, making them a part of your morning rituals or bedtime reflections. Allow them to weave into the tapestry of your thoughts, transforming self-limiting beliefs into empowering statements of confidence and possibility.

Remember that affirmations are not mere words; they are the keys that unlock the doors to success and fulfillment. Embrace them with unwavering faith and determination, for as you do, you will witness the extraordinary power of repetition—the force that shapes beliefs, molds mindsets, and ushers you towards a life of remarkable achievements.

Chapter of Overcoming Challenges

Phrases to Strengthen Resilience and Conquer Obstacles

Life, like a magnificent journey, presents us with a myriad of challenges—tests of our strength, resilience, and determination. In this chapter, we delve into the art of overcoming challenges, equipping ourselves with powerful phrases that ignite the flames of courage and fortitude within us. With each phrase repeated, we reinforce the belief that within us lies the power to rise above adversity and triumph over every obstacle that crosses our path.

Exercise 1: Embracing Resilience

"I am resilient, and I bounce back from adversity stronger than ever."
"Challenges are opportunities for growth, and I welcome them with courage."
"I trust in my ability to handle whatever life throws my way."

Exercise 2: Conquering Fear

"I face my fears with bravery, knowing they hold no power over me."
"I release the grip of fear and embrace the freedom of bold action."
"I am capable of handling uncertainty and stepping into the unknown."

Exercise 3: Finding Solutions

"I am resourceful and creative in finding solutions to every challenge."
"I approach obstacles with a calm and clear mind, ready to conquer them."
"No challenge is insurmountable; I trust in my problem-solving abilities."

Exercise 4: Cultivating Determination

"I persist in the face of setbacks, knowing they are stepping stones to success."
"I am unwavering in my pursuit of my goals and dreams."
"I am dedicated to my vision, and I persevere with unwavering determination."

Exercise 5: Embracing Change

"I welcome change as a catalyst for growth and transformation."
"I adapt easily to new circumstances, finding strength in flexibility."
"With each change, I discover new opportunities for success."

Exercise 6: Trusting in Divine Timing

"I trust in the flow of life, knowing that everything happens for a reason."
"Divine timing guides my path, and I am patient as I await the perfect moment."
"Even in challenges, I find comfort in the greater plan that unfolds before me."

Exercise 7: Embracing Positive Mindset

"I replace negative thoughts with empowering beliefs."
"I maintain a positive outlook, even in the face of adversity."
"Optimism is my guiding light, illuminating the darkest moments."

Exercise 8: Celebrating Personal Growth

"Each challenge I overcome is a testament to my strength and resilience."
"I am proud of the person I am becoming through every experience."
"Through challenges, I discover my true potential and embrace growth."

As you repeat these phrases, feel the surge of strength and courage within you. Let them be the battle cries that embolden your spirit, helping you conquer challenges and emerge triumphant on the other side. Embrace these affirmations not only as words but as profound declarations of your ability to rise above any obstacle.

In times of struggle, return to these phrases as a wellspring of inspiration, rekindling the fire of determination within you. Allow them to be your allies, guiding you through adversity with grace and resilience.

Remember, challenges are not barriers but opportunities for growth and transformation. With every obstacle overcome, you emerge stronger, wiser, and more empowered to face whatever lies ahead. Armed with these phrases, you possess the tools to embrace challenges with a warrior's spirit, secure in the knowledge that within you beats the heart of a champion—a soul ready to rise above every obstacle and claim victory on the journey of life.

Chapter of Positive Relationships

Repetitive exercises for fostering healthy connections and communication

In the tapestry of life, our relationships weave the most intricate and colorful patterns, adding depth and meaning to our existence. This chapter is dedicated to the art of fostering positive relationships—a canvas upon which we create bonds of love, trust, and understanding. Through a series of repetitive exercises, we shall nurture the seeds of empathy and compassion, cultivating healthy connections and open communication with the people we cherish.

Exercise 1: Cultivating Empathy

"I practice active listening, giving my full attention to others without judgment."
"I empathize with the feelings and experiences of those around me."
"I treat others with kindness and compassion, for we all carry our own burdens."

Exercise 2: Expressing Gratitude

"I express gratitude and appreciation for the people in my life."
"I cherish the relationships I have and let others know they are valued."
"I am thankful for the love and support I receive, and I reciprocate it wholeheartedly."

Exercise 3: Setting Boundaries with Love

"I communicate my boundaries with clarity and respect."
"I honor the boundaries of others, understanding that it nurtures healthy connections."
"Setting boundaries is an act of self-care and love for both myself and others."

Exercise 4: Resolving Conflict with Understanding

"I approach conflicts with an open heart and a willingness to understand."
"I seek common ground and collaborate to find resolutions that benefit all."
"Conflict is an opportunity for growth and strengthening relationships."

Exercise 5: Practicing Positive Communication

"I choose my words wisely, speaking with kindness and honesty."
"I am mindful of my tone and body language, ensuring my message is received positively."
"Positive communication is the key to fostering deeper connections."

Exercise 6: Celebrating Individuality

"I celebrate the uniqueness of each person in my life."
"I respect the differences that make our relationships diverse and enriching."
"Embracing individuality enhances the beauty of our connections."

Exercise 7: Nurturing Supportive Relationships

"I surround myself with people who uplift and support me."
"I am a source of encouragement and support for my loved ones."
"I create a circle of trust and care, fostering an environment of love and understanding."

Exercise 8: Practicing Forgiveness and Grace

"I forgive others with compassion and release the weight of resentment."
"I am open to receiving forgiveness and grace when I make mistakes."
"Forgiveness is a gift I give to myself and others, freeing us to grow together."

As you repeat these exercises, allow them to sink deeply into your heart and soul. Embrace them with the understanding that fostering positive relationships is a continuous practice—a journey of growth, learning, and connection.

Integrate these exercises into your daily interactions, making them a part of your communication and expression of love. As you do, you will witness the transformation of your relationships—a harmonious symphony of understanding, support, and appreciation.

Remember, the beauty of positive relationships lies not only in what you receive but in what you give. As you cultivate empathy, gratitude, and open communication, you contribute to a world rich in love and understanding. With each repetitive exercise, you strengthen the bonds that tie us together, creating a tapestry of positive relationships that will enrich your life and the lives of those you touch.

Chapter of Abundance and Prosperity

Techniques to shift scarcity mindset into one of abundance

In the vast expanse of the universe, abundance flows like a river, carrying with it the bountiful gifts of life. This chapter is dedicated to unlocking the gates to abundance and prosperity —a journey that begins with the transformation of a scarcity mindset into one of abundance and possibility. Through a series of empowering techniques, we shall rewire our thoughts, align our beliefs, and embrace the abundance that awaits us.

Technique 1: Gratitude for the Present

Practice daily gratitude for the abundance that already exists in your life. Count your blessings and acknowledge the abundance of love, health, and opportunities that surround you. Embrace the fullness of the present moment, appreciating the richness it holds.

Technique 2: Abundance Affirmations

Repeat affirmations that affirm abundance and prosperity. Let these phrases echo in your mind and heart:

"I attract abundance and prosperity into my life effortlessly."
"I am worthy of abundance in all areas of my life."
"Opportunities for success flow to me abundantly."

Technique 3: Visualization of Abundance

Create a vivid mental picture of the abundance you desire. Visualize your life filled with prosperity, envisioning the goals you want to achieve, the experiences you wish to have, and the abundance that surrounds you. Immerse yourself in this vision, allowing it to fuel your motivation and belief in the abundance that is possible for you.

Technique 4: Embrace the Law of Attraction

Understand and embrace the Law of Attraction—the principle that like attracts like. Focus your thoughts and energy on abundance, and you will attract more abundance into your life. Release thoughts of scarcity and lack, replacing them with positive, abundant thoughts and beliefs.

Technique 5: Generosity and Abundance

Practice acts of generosity, giving without expectation. Embrace the abundance mindset that there is more than enough to share. By being generous, you signal to the universe your belief in abundance, creating a cycle of giving and receiving.

Technique 6: Shift from Scarcity to Gratitude

When scarcity thoughts arise, consciously shift your focus to gratitude. Replace thoughts of lack with thoughts of abundance and appreciation. Cultivate a mindset of abundance by redirecting your thoughts towards the abundance that is available to you.

Technique 7: Celebrate Others' Success

Celebrate the success of others without envy or comparison. Acknowledge that their success does not diminish your own, as abundance is limitless. Embrace the belief that there is enough success and prosperity for everyone.

Technique 8: Abundance Journaling

Create an abundance journal to record the abundance and prosperity that flows into your life. Write about the opportunities, blessings, and positive experiences you encounter. Review your journal regularly to reinforce your belief in abundance.

As you engage in these techniques, remember that abundance is a state of mind, not just a material possession. Embrace the abundance of love, joy, and opportunities that exist beyond material wealth. Embody the belief that the universe is abundant, and you are deserving of the abundance it offers.

Chapter of Health and Well-being

Repetition for promoting physical and mental wellness

In the temple of our body and mind, health and well-being are the sacred foundations upon which we build a fulfilling and vibrant life. This chapter is devoted to the art of nurturing our physical and mental wellness—a journey that begins with the gentle cadence of repetition. Through a series of empowering phrases, we shall cultivate habits of self-care, mindfulness, and positive thinking, fostering a holistic state of well-being that nourishes our body, mind, and soul.

Repetition 1: Self-Care as a Priority

"I prioritize self-care as an essential part of my daily routine."
"Nurturing myself is an act of love and respect for my well-being."
"I listen to my body's needs and honor them with self-compassion."

Repetition 2: Embracing Mindful Practices

"I practice mindfulness to anchor myself in the present moment."
"With each breath, I cultivate a sense of calm and centeredness."
"I let go of worries and fears, embracing the serenity of the now."

Repetition 3: Positive Affirmations for Physical Health

"My body is a temple, and I treat it with reverence and care."
"I am committed to making healthy choices that nourish my body."
"With each healthy choice, I invest in my long-term well-being."

Repetition 4: Cultivating Mental Resilience

"I face challenges with mental strength and unwavering resilience."
"I replace negative thoughts with empowering and positive beliefs."
"My mind is a sanctuary of peace and clarity, free from self-doubt."

Repetition 5: Gratitude for Well-being

"I am grateful for my body's ability to heal and thrive."
"I express gratitude for my mental clarity and emotional balance."
"I cherish my overall well-being as a precious gift to treasure."

Repetition 6: Daily Movement and Exercise

"I embrace the joy of movement and the vitality it brings to my life."
"Each day, I make time for physical activity to nurture my body."
"Exercise is a celebration of my strength and energy."

Repetition 7: Mind-Body Connection

"I honor the powerful connection between my mind and body."
"I listen to my body's signals and respond with loving care."
"Through mind-body harmony, I cultivate balance and well-being."

Repetition 8: Inner Peace and Serenity

"I find solace in moments of quiet reflection and inner peace."
"I release stress and tension, allowing tranquility to flow within me."
"Serenity is my birthright, and I embrace it with an open heart."

As you repeat these phrases, immerse yourself in their essence, feeling their transformative power ripple through your being. Embrace them as the mantras that guide your journey to physical and mental wellness—a journey of self-discovery and nurturing.

Integrate these repetitions into your daily life, infusing your routines with mindfulness, self-care, and gratitude. With each repetition, you cultivate a resilient and balanced state of well-being, fostering a sanctuary of health within you.

Chapter of Confidence and Courage

Building unshakable self-assurance through affirmations

In the grand theater of life, confidence and courage are the twin stars that illuminate our path to greatness. This chapter is dedicated to cultivating unshakable self-assurance—a journey that begins with the empowering cadence of affirmations. Through a series of bold and empowering phrases, we shall fortify our belief in ourselves, igniting the flames of confidence and courage that reside within our hearts.

Affirmation 1: Embracing My Authenticity

"I am authentic and unapologetically true to myself."
"I embrace my uniqueness as a source of strength and beauty."
"I radiate confidence, knowing that I am enough just as I am."

Affirmation 2: Trusting in My Abilities

"I trust in my abilities to overcome any challenge that comes my way."
"I am capable, resourceful, and resilient in the face of adversity."
"I believe in my skills and talents, and I use them to create success."

Affirmation 3: Letting Go of Self-Doubt

"I release self-doubt and replace it with unwavering self-assurance."
"I am not defined by my past mistakes; I am defined by my growth."
"I deserve success and happiness, and I embrace them with open arms."

Affirmation 4: Embracing Courageous Action

"I act with courage and boldness, seizing opportunities fearlessly."
"I step outside my comfort zone, knowing it is where true growth lies."
"Every step I take is a courageous leap towards my dreams."

Affirmation 5: Believing in My Vision

"I have a clear vision for my life, and I am unwavering in its pursuit."
"My dreams are attainable, and I create a plan to make them a reality."
"I trust in the journey, knowing that each step brings me closer to my vision."

Affirmation 6: Celebrating My Accomplishments

"I celebrate my achievements with pride and gratitude."
"I recognize my progress and growth, no matter how small."
"I am deserving of praise and acknowledgment for my efforts."

Affirmation 7: Embracing Positive Self-Talk

"I replace negative self-talk with words of encouragement and empowerment."
"I speak to myself with kindness and compassion, like a supportive friend."
"I am my own cheerleader, lifting myself up with positivity and love."

Affirmation 8: Radiating Confidence

"I am a beacon of confidence, inspiring others with my self-assurance."
"I exude charisma and poise, attracting success and positive opportunities."
"My self-assurance empowers me to lead with authenticity and grace."

As you repeat these affirmations, let them reverberate through the core of your being. Embrace them with unwavering faith, for they are the seeds that blossom into unshakable self-assurance. With each repetition, you awaken the mighty force of confidence and courage within you, propelling you towards greatness.

Integrate these affirmations into your daily rituals, anchoring them in your morning reflections or bedtime meditations. Let them be the compass that guides your actions and thoughts, empowering you to conquer every challenge with grace and fortitude.

Chapter of Focus and Productivity

Techniques to stay focused, organized and productive

In the tapestry of time, focus and productivity are the threads that weave the fabric of success and fulfillment. This chapter is dedicated to the art of honing our focus, mastering organization, and embracing productivity—a journey that begins with the adoption of empowering techniques. Through a series of mindful practices and strategies, we shall unlock the door to heightened concentration, efficiency, and accomplishment.

Technique 1: Mindful Prioritization

"I prioritize my tasks based on their importance and impact."
"I focus on high-value activities that align with my goals."
"I allocate time and attention to tasks that bring the greatest results."

Technique 2: Time Blocking

"I divide my day into focused time blocks for specific tasks."
"During each time block, I immerse myself fully in the task at hand."
"I respect my schedule and stay committed to each time block."

Technique 3: Eliminating Distractions

"I create a distraction-free environment to enhance my focus."
"I turn off notifications and set boundaries for interruptions."
"I stay present and fully engaged in my work, disregarding distractions."

Technique 4: Setting S.M.A.R.T. Goals

"I set Specific, Measurable, Achievable, Relevant, and Time-bound goals."
"My goals provide clear direction and purpose to my actions."
"I break down larger goals into smaller, manageable tasks."

Technique 5: Utilizing To-Do Lists

"I maintain a to-do list to keep track of my tasks and commitments."
"I regularly review and update my list to stay organized."
"Crossing off completed tasks fills me with a sense of accomplishment."

Technique 6: Mindful Breaks and Rest

"I take short breaks to recharge and maintain mental clarity."
"I prioritize self-care, ensuring adequate rest and rejuvenation."
"I return to my work with renewed focus and energy after breaks."

Technique 7: Single-Tasking

"I embrace single-tasking, devoting my full attention to one task at a time."
"I avoid multitasking, recognizing its impact on focus and efficiency."
"Through single-tasking, I produce higher-quality work in less time."

Technique 8: Reflecting and Learning

"I regularly reflect on my progress and identify areas for improvement."
"I learn from my experiences, adapting and growing with each challenge."
"Continuous improvement is the key to achieving higher levels of productivity."

As you practice these techniques, let them become ingrained habits that transform your approach to work and life. Embrace them with intention and mindfulness, for they are the building blocks of focus and productivity—the keys to unlocking your fullest potential.

Integrate these techniques into your daily routine, ensuring they become an integral part of your journey towards success. As you do, you will witness the remarkable transformation of your productivity—an evolution of efficiency, focus, and accomplishment.

Chapter of Letting Go

Exercises to release negative emotions and past baggage

In the vast expanse of our hearts, lies the liberation that comes with letting go—the art of releasing negative emotions and shedding the weight of past baggage. This chapter is dedicated to the journey of healing and freedom—a path paved with transformative exercises that liberate us from the chains of the past. Through a series of empowering practices, we shall embrace the power of forgiveness, self-compassion, and acceptance, setting ourselves free to embrace the beauty of the present.

Exercise 1: Emotional Release Journaling

Write a heartfelt letter to yourself or someone else to express any pent-up emotions or grievances. Pour your emotions onto paper without judgment, allowing the words to flow freely. Afterward, release the emotions by tearing up or burning the letter as a symbolic act of letting go.

Exercise 2: Forgiveness Meditation

Engage in a forgiveness meditation to release any resentments or grudges. Visualize the person you need to forgive, and say these words:

"I release you and myself from the burden of past hurts."
"I forgive you, and I set us both free to heal and grow."

Feel the weight of negativity lifting from your heart as you extend forgiveness to others and yourself.

Exercise 3: Releasing Physical Tension

Practice progressive muscle relaxation or deep breathing exercises to release physical tension held in your body. With each exhale, imagine letting go of stress and negative energy, feeling lighter and more at peace with each breath.

Exercise 4: Mindful Acceptance

Practice mindfulness and self-compassion, acknowledging and accepting any painful emotions or experiences without judgment. Recognize that it's okay to feel these emotions and that they don't define you. Embrace self-compassion, treating yourself with kindness and understanding.

Exercise 5: Visualization of Release

Close your eyes and visualize a box in front of you. Mentally place your past baggage and negative emotions into the box. As you visualize doing this, see the box being lifted away from you, floating further and further into the distance until it disappears completely. Feel a sense of relief and lightness as you let go.

Exercise 6: Symbolic Ritual of Release

Create a symbolic ritual to mark your letting go. This could involve writing down negative emotions on paper and burying them in the ground or releasing them into a flowing river. The act of physically letting go in a symbolic way can be deeply therapeutic.

Exercise 7: Affirmations of Release

Repeat affirmations that reinforce your commitment to letting go:

"I release the past and embrace the present with an open heart."
"I let go of what no longer serves me and make space for new possibilities."
"I am free from the weight of the past, and I walk into the future with lightness and grace."

Exercise 8: Engaging in Creative Expression

Express your emotions through art, writing, or any creative outlet that resonates with you. Creativity can be a powerful way to release and process emotions, allowing you to find healing and closure.

As you engage in these exercises, be gentle with yourself, for letting go is a process of healing and self-discovery. Embrace these practices with an open heart and an intention to free yourself from the burden of the past.

May this chapter be an invitation to embark on the journey of letting go—a testament to the transformative power of releasing negative emotions and past baggage. As you walk this path of healing and liberation, you will find yourself stepping into the radiant light of the present—a space where you can breathe freely, embrace self-compassion, and live with the profound wisdom of having learned to let go.

Chapter of Joy and Happiness

Repetitive phrases to embrace joy and cultivate happiness

In the garden of our souls, joy and happiness bloom like vibrant flowers, enriching our lives with beauty and meaning. This chapter is dedicated to nurturing the seeds of joy and cultivating the essence of happiness—a journey that begins with the repetition of empowering phrases. Through a series of heartfelt affirmations, we shall immerse ourselves in the splendor of joy, basking in the radiance of happiness that dwells within.

Repetition 1: Embracing Joy in the Present

"I find joy in the simple pleasures of each day."
"I embrace the beauty around me, finding joy in the little things."
"Each moment is an opportunity to experience joy and gratitude."

Repetition 2: Choosing Happiness

"I choose happiness as my companion on this journey of life."
"I am worthy of happiness and deserving of a joyful existence."
"I prioritize my happiness and cultivate it with intention."

Repetition 3: Gratitude for Happiness

"I am grateful for the happiness that fills my heart and soul."
"I express gratitude for the moments of joy that brighten my life."
"Embracing gratitude magnifies the happiness within me."

Repetition 4: Self-Love and Happiness

"I love and accept myself, cultivating a foundation of happiness."
"I radiate happiness from within, nourishing my spirit."
"Self-love is the key to unlocking the gates to happiness."

Repetition 5: Spreading Joy to Others

"I spread joy to others with acts of kindness and compassion."
"The more joy I give, the more it multiplies within me."
"Bringing joy to others fills my heart with boundless happiness."

Repetition 6: Living in the Present

"I release worries of the past and anxieties of the future."
"I find joy in the present moment, savoring life's blessings."
"Happiness blossoms in the soil of presence and mindfulness."

Repetition 7: Joyful Affirmations

"I attract joy and happiness into my life effortlessly."
"I am the creator of my own happiness, and I choose joy every day."
"Happiness is my birthright, and I claim it with an open heart."

Repetition 8: Embodying the Spirit of Joy

"I am a vessel of joy, allowing it to radiate through me."
"Joyful energy flows through my actions and interactions."
"Embodying joy uplifts those around me, creating a ripple of happiness."

As you repeat these phrases, let them reverberate through the depths of your being. Embrace them as the mantras that invite joy and happiness into your life—a symphony of positivity and fulfillment. With each repetition, you cultivate a mindset that celebrates the gift of joy and cherishes the essence of happiness.

Integrate these affirmations into your daily rituals, allowing them to be the guiding stars that lead you towards a life of joy and contentment. As you do, you will witness the remarkable transformation—a life illuminated by the brilliance of joy, radiating happiness to yourself and all those whose lives you touch.

Chapter of Purpose and Passion

Techniques to discover and pursue your life's purpose

In the vast canvas of existence, purpose and passion paint the colors of our journey, infusing our lives with meaning and fulfillment. This chapter is dedicated to the art of uncovering your life's purpose—a quest that sets your heart on fire with unwavering passion. Through a series of soul-searching techniques, we shall explore the depths of your being, guiding you towards the revelation of your purpose and igniting the flame of your true calling.

Technique 1: Reflecting on Core Values

Explore your core values—the principles that define what is most important to you. Reflect on the values that resonate deeply within your soul, aligning your actions and choices with these guiding stars.

Technique 2: Identifying Natural Talents and Skills

Take an inventory of your natural talents and skills. Observe the activities that come effortlessly to you, where time seems to stand still. Your purpose may lie in the intersection of your passions and innate abilities.

Technique 3: Listening to Your Inner Voice

Engage in mindfulness and introspection, quieting the noise around you to listen to the whispers of your inner voice. Tune into your intuition and inner wisdom, for they carry the profound messages that guide you towards your purpose.

Technique 4: Exploring Past Experiences

Examine significant moments and experiences in your life. Look for patterns or themes that emerge from these experiences, as they may hold clues to your purpose and passions.

Technique 5: Seeking Inspiration from Role Models

Study the lives of individuals who inspire you. Observe how their journeys align with their purpose and passion. Their stories may offer insights and motivation as you explore your own path.

Technique 6: Embracing Curiosity and Exploration

Cultivate a sense of curiosity and openness to new experiences. Engage in different activities, travel, and seek opportunities to learn and grow. The exploration of new territories may lead you closer to your purpose.

Technique 7: Embracing the Fear of Uncertainty

Acknowledge and embrace the fear of uncertainty that accompanies the pursuit of purpose. Embrace it as a natural part of the journey, and let it guide you towards the path that feels authentic and true.

Technique 8: Journaling for Clarity

Keep a journal to record your thoughts, feelings, and reflections on your purpose-seeking journey. Writing can bring clarity and insight, allowing you to better understand your desires and aspirations.

As you engage in these techniques, be patient and compassionate with yourself. The discovery of your life's purpose is a profound journey that unfolds over time. Embrace the process, knowing that each step brings you closer to aligning your life with your true calling.

Chapter of Resilience and Growth

Building inner strength and embracing personal growth

In the crucible of life, resilience and growth forge a powerful alchemy, transforming challenges into opportunities for inner strength and evolution. This chapter is dedicated to the art of cultivating resilience—a journey that empowers you to rise above adversity—and embracing personal growth—a path that nurtures your evolution into the best version of yourself. Through a series of empowering practices, we shall fortify your spirit, nurture your self-belief, and embrace the transformative power of growth.

Practice 1: Embracing Change as an Ally

"I welcome change as a catalyst for growth and transformation."
"I adapt easily to new circumstances, finding strength in flexibility."
"With each change, I discover new opportunities for resilience."

Practice 2: Turning Setbacks into Stepping Stones

"I see setbacks as stepping stones to success and growth."
"Each challenge I overcome is a testament to my resilience."
"I am not defined by my failures; I am defined by how I rise from them."

Practice 3: Cultivating a Growth Mindset

"I believe in my ability to learn and improve in every situation."
"I embrace challenges as opportunities to expand my capabilities."
"I view failures as valuable lessons that propel me forward."

Practice 4: Practicing Self-Compassion

"I treat myself with kindness and understanding in times of difficulty."
"I acknowledge that it's okay to struggle; it's a natural part of growth."
"I extend the same compassion to myself as I would to a dear friend."

Practice 5: Finding Strength in Adversity

"I draw upon my inner strength to face challenges with courage."
"Adversity is an opportunity for me to tap into my resilience."
"I trust in my ability to handle whatever life presents to me."

Practice 6: Mindful Reflection and Learning

"I engage in mindful reflection to uncover the lessons in every experience."
"I learn from both successes and failures, gaining wisdom from each."
"Every step I take is an opportunity for growth and self-discovery."

Practice 7: Celebrating Personal Growth

"I celebrate my progress and growth with gratitude and joy."
"I recognize that personal growth is a lifelong journey of evolution."
"Each day, I become a better version of myself, step by step."

Practice 8: Embracing Resilient Optimism

"I maintain a positive outlook, even in the face of challenges."
"I focus on solutions and possibilities rather than dwelling on problems."
"Optimism is my guiding light, illuminating the darkest moments."

As you engage in these practices, remember that resilience and growth are lifelong companions on your journey. Embrace them with unwavering faith in your capacity to evolve, learn, and thrive.

Integrate these practices into your daily life, making them a part of your mindset and approach to challenges. Embrace resilience as your shield, guarding you from despair, and growth as your wings, lifting you higher on the winds of transformation.

Chapter of Visualizing Success

Utilizing repetition to enhance the power of visualization

In the realm of dreams and aspirations, visualization holds the key to unlocking the doors of success. This chapter is dedicated to the art of visualizing success—a journey that begins with the repetitive practice of empowering imagery. Through a series of immersive visualizations, we shall harness the power of repetition to strengthen our mental images, align our focus, and pave the path towards achieving our goals.

Visualization 1: The Clarity of Intent

Repeatedly visualize your goals with utmost clarity and specificity. See yourself achieving your dreams in vivid detail—the sights, sounds, and emotions of success. The more defined and detailed your mental images, the more real they become.

Visualization 2: Embracing the Feeling of Achievement

Engage all your senses to immerse yourself in the feeling of achievement. Experience the rush of pride and joy that comes with reaching your goals. The more you feel the emotions of success, the more your subconscious mind accepts it as reality.

Visualization 3: Overcoming Obstacles with Resilience

Replay mental scenarios where you encounter challenges and overcome them with resilience and determination. Visualize yourself navigating through obstacles, finding creative solutions, and emerging victorious. This practice strengthens your belief in your ability to overcome any hurdles that may arise.

Visualization 4: Embodying Confidence and Self-Belief

Repeatedly visualize yourself exuding confidence and self-assuredness. See yourself radiating with belief in your skills and capabilities. Embrace the image of yourself as a successful and confident individual, for this self-belief becomes a powerful magnet for achieving your goals.

Visualization 5: Savoring the Journey of Success

Visualize not only the destination but also the journey towards success. See yourself progressing, growing, and learning with each step. Embrace the joy of the process, as this joy fuels your motivation and commitment.

Visualization 6: Affirming Your Success

Accompany your visualizations with empowering affirmations:

"I am worthy of success and capable of achieving my goals."
"I embrace the vision of success and work diligently to make it a reality."
"With each repetition, my visualizations grow stronger, guiding me towards success."

Visualization 7: Practicing Visualization Regularly

Incorporate daily visualization sessions into your routine. Consistency is key to enhancing the power of visualization. Dedicate time each day to immerse yourself in the mental imagery of success.

Visualization 8: Integrating Visualization with Action

Combine your visualizations with purposeful action. As you visualize success, take tangible steps towards your goals. The synergy between visualization and action accelerates your progress.

As you engage in these visualizations, embrace them with unwavering faith in the power of your mind to shape your reality. With each repetition, you strengthen the connection between your mind and your goals, aligning your subconscious with your conscious intentions.

Conclusion

Reflecting on Your Mindset Journey

As we reach the conclusion of this book, it is time to pause and reflect on the magnificent journey of cultivating a positive and successful mindset. Throughout these pages, we have explored the transformative power of repetition, mindfulness, and visualization—the tools that empower us to shape our beliefs, enhance our focus, and manifest our aspirations. We have delved into the realms of resilience, joy, purpose, and more, uncovering the essential elements that contribute to a fulfilling and purposeful life.

In our exploration of the mind's workings, we discovered the profound impact of repetition in rewiring our beliefs and behaviors. Repetitive phrases have the remarkable ability to shape our thoughts, inspiring us to embrace self-compassion, confidence, and the pursuit of our dreams. The art of repetition became the cornerstone of our mindset journey, guiding us towards a state of inner strength and empowerment.

Embracing Mindfulness allowed us to anchor ourselves in the present moment, freeing us from the shackles of the past and the anxieties of the future. Through mindfulness, we found peace, acceptance, and a deeper connection with ourselves and the world around us. Mindfulness became our compass, leading us towards a life of gratitude, serenity, and self-awareness.

The Science of Repetition and Neuroplasticity revealed the remarkable adaptability of our brains, reminding us that change is possible at any stage of life. Our beliefs are not fixed; they are malleable. With the repetition of empowering phrases, we rewired our neural pathways, opening the door to personal growth, resilience, and transformation.

We embarked on the pursuit of Purpose and Passion, seeking to uncover the threads that weave the fabric of our unique life's purpose. Through introspection and exploration, we embraced our core values, passions, and natural talents, aligning our actions with our true calling.

Resilience and Growth became our allies in the face of challenges and setbacks. We learned to view adversity as an opportunity for growth and self-discovery, cultivating an unwavering belief in our ability to rise above obstacles and flourish.

The pursuit of Joy and Happiness reminded us that happiness is not a destination but a state of mind. By embracing gratitude, self-love, and the power of positive affirmations, we unlocked the gates to a joyful existence, radiating happiness from within.

In Visualizing Success, we harnessed the power of our imagination to paint vibrant images of achievement and abundance. Through the repetition of vivid mental imagery, we cultivated self-belief, resilience, and unwavering determination, propelling us towards the realization of our goals.

The Path of Letting Go taught us the transformative art of releasing negative emotions and past baggage. Through forgiveness, self-compassion, and symbolic rituals, we liberated ourselves from the burdens of the past, making space for growth, healing, and a lighter heart.

The Role of Mindset in Success underscored the profound impact our mindset has on our achievements. By adopting a growth mindset and embracing the power of positive thinking, we became architects of our success, harnessing our thoughts and beliefs to shape our reality.

Emphasizing the Importance of Continued Practice

As we conclude this journey, it is essential to remember that mindset work is not a destination but an ongoing practice. Just as we exercise to strengthen our bodies, we must continue to nurture and develop our minds. The power of repetition lies in its consistency, and the power of mindfulness comes from regular practice. Embrace the repetition of empowering phrases, continue to practice mindfulness, and maintain your visualization sessions.

As you encounter challenges or setbacks, draw upon the resilience you have cultivated. Celebrate your growth, embrace change, and trust in your ability to learn and adapt. Remember that your mindset is not fixed, and you have the power to shape it for a life of fulfillment, success, and happiness.

The journey of cultivating a positive and successful mindset is a lifelong adventure—an exploration of self-discovery, empowerment, and transformation. With each step, you unveil the masterpiece of your true potential—a tapestry of beliefs, passions, and aspirations that weave together to create the magnificent symphony of your life.

May this book serve as a guiding light on your continued journey of mindset growth and evolution. As you embrace the power of repetition, mindfulness, and visualization, may you walk confidently towards the life you envision—a life of purpose, resilience, joy, and achievement. Trust in the strength of your mindset, for it holds the key to unlocking the abundance of possibilities that await you on your remarkable journey of self-discovery and empowerment.

Gratitude to the Pioneering Minds

Thanking the Famous Authors Who Unveiled the Secrets of Mindset and Success

In the vast landscape of knowledge and wisdom, we stand on the shoulders of giants—famous authors whose groundbreaking discoveries have illuminated the path to a positive and successful mindset. As we conclude this journey, it is with profound gratitude and admiration that we pay tribute to these pioneering minds. Their insights and teachings have paved the way for our exploration of resilience, purpose, visualization, and the transformative power of repetition. Let us express our heartfelt thanks to these luminaries who have enriched our lives with their wisdom.

<u>Carol Dweck</u>: With her pioneering research on the growth mindset, Carol Dweck taught us that our beliefs about our abilities significantly impact our achievements. We are grateful for her invaluable contribution to the understanding that embracing a growth mindset is the key to unlocking our full potential.

<u>Jon Kabat-Zinn</u>: Through his work on mindfulness-based stress reduction, Jon Kabat-Zinn showed us the profound impact of mindfulness on our mental and emotional well-being. We express our gratitude for his teachings that have guided us towards greater self-awareness and inner peace.

<u>Napoleon Hill</u>: In his timeless work "Think and Grow Rich," Napoleon Hill laid the foundation for understanding the power of our thoughts in shaping our reality. We thank him for illuminating the path to abundance, success, and the importance of a positive mental attitude.

Louise Hay: With her groundbreaking teachings on the power of affirmations and self-love, Louise Hay gifted us the tools to transform our beliefs and embrace self-compassion. We are grateful for her profound impact on our journey towards self-empowerment and healing.

Viktor Frankl: In his masterpiece "Man's Search for Meaning," Viktor Frankl revealed the profound resilience of the human spirit and the importance of finding purpose even in the face of unimaginable adversity. We express our gratitude for his inspiration to discover meaning in our lives.

Shawn Achor: Through his research on positive psychology and the science of happiness, Shawn Achor enlightened us about the connection between positivity, success, and well-being. We thank him for showing us the importance of cultivating joy and gratitude in our daily lives.

Stephen Covey: In "The 7 Habits of Highly Effective People," Stephen Covey shared timeless principles for personal effectiveness and growth. We express our gratitude for his guidance in aligning our actions with our values and striving for continuous improvement.

Eckhart Tolle: Through his transformative teachings on presence and the power of now, Eckhart Tolle guided us towards a deeper understanding of mindfulness and spiritual awakening. We are thankful for his wisdom that has opened our eyes to the beauty of the present moment.

Deepak Chopra: With his profound insights into mind-body healing and spirituality, Deepak Chopra expanded our understanding of the interconnectedness of our well-being. We express our gratitude for his teachings that have inspired us to embrace holistic growth.

Gabrielle Bernstein: Through her work on self-love and spiritual growth, Gabrielle Bernstein taught us the importance of cultivating inner peace and finding strength in vulnerability. We thank her for guiding us towards a deeper connection with our true selves.

To all the authors, thinkers, and visionaries who have contributed to our understanding of mindset and success, we offer our heartfelt gratitude. Your teachings have shaped the very foundation of this book, empowering us to embark on a transformative journey of self-discovery, growth, and empowerment.

The Secret of Positive and Successful Mindset
Copyright ©2023 Lucas Oliver Williams
All rights reserved.

Reproduction of any content in this publication is strictly prohibited unless written permission is obtained from the publisher. The only exception is for brief quotes included in critical articles or reviews. The photos used in the book are licensed under Canva Pro.

Milton Keynes UK
Ingram Content Group UK Ltd.
UKHW022316050923
428126UK00006B/164